Disaster Diaries

Surviving the WILDFIRE

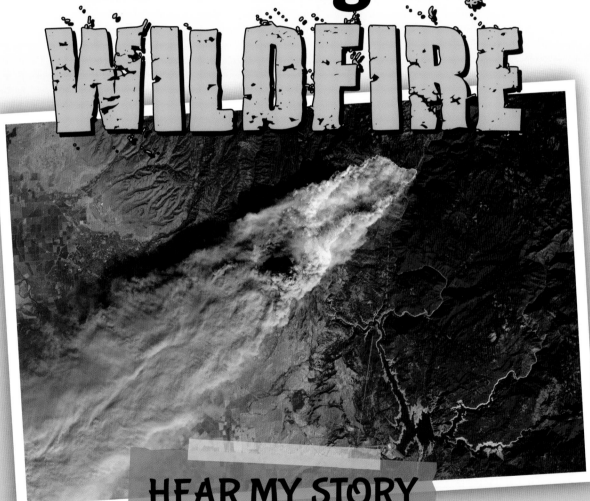

HEAR MY STORY

Sarah Eason

CRABTREE
PUBLISHING COMPANY
WWW.CRABTREEBOOKS.COM

Author: Sarah Eason

Editorial director: Kathy Middleton

Editors: Jennifer Sanderson and Ellen Rodger

Proofreaders: Tracey Kelly, Melissa Boyce

Editorial director: Kathy Middleton

Design: Paul Myerscough

Cover design: Margaret Amy Salter

Photo research: Rachel Blount

Production coordinator and
   Prepress technician: Tammy McGarr

Print coordinator: Katherine Berti

Consultant: John Farndon

Produced for Crabtree Publishing Company by Calcium

Photo Credits:
t=Top, c=Center, b=Bottom, l= Left, r=Right

Inside: Shutterstock: Aapsky: p. 25; Alexpunker: p. 21; Bruno Ismael Silva Alves: p. 10; ARM Photo Video: p. 20; B.A.Beard: p. 23t; Bilanol: p. 4; BrittanyNY: p. 5; Volodymyr Burdiak: p. 8; ChrisVanLennepPhoto: p. 26; ElRoce: pp. 1, 17l; Sheila Fitzgerald: pp. 22-23; N K: pp. 28-29; Mitchell Krog: p. 19t; Tina Lawhon: pp. 6-7; Rich Lonardo: pp. 16-17; Mc_Mon: p. 15; Dylan Mittag: pp. 12-13; Jamen Percy: pp. 18-19b; Thavon Phumijan: p. 13t; Vlad Teodor: p. 9; Eugene R Thieszen: p. 24; Toa55: p. 11; Nils Versemann: p. 27; M Yerman: p. 29r; Zelenkoff: p. 14.

Cover: flickr: USDA Forest Service

Publisher's Note: The story presented in this book is a fictional account based on extensive research of real-life accounts, with the aim of reflecting the true experience of victims of natural disasters.

Library and Archives Canada Cataloguing in Publication

Title: Surviving the wildfire : hear my story / Sarah Eason.
Names: Eason, Sarah, author.
Description: Series statement: Disaster diaries | Includes index.
Identifiers: Canadiana (print) 20200150200 |
   Canadiana (ebook) 20200150219 |
   ISBN 9780778771111 (hardcover) |
   ISBN 9780778771210 (softcover) |
   ISBN 9781427124500 (HTML)
Subjects: LCSH: Wildfires—California—Paradise—Juvenile literature.
   | LCSH: Wildfires—Juvenile literature. | LCSH: Disaster victims—
   Juvenile literature.
Classification: LCC SD421.23 .E27 2020 | DDC j363.37/9—dc23

Library of Congress Cataloging-in-Publication Data

Names: Eason, Sarah, author.
Title: Surviving the wildfire : hear my story / Sarah Eason.
Description: New York : Crabtree Publishing Company, [2020] |
   Series: Disaster diaries | Includes bibliographical references and
   index.
Identifiers: LCCN 2019053369 (print) |
   LCCN 2019053370 (ebook) |
   ISBN 9780778771111 (hardcover) | ISBN 9780778771210 (paperback) |
   ISBN 9781427124500 (ebook)
Subjects: LCSH: Robertson, Toni (Wildfire survivor)--Juvenile
   literature. | Wildfires--California--Paradise--Juvenile literature. |
   Wildfires--Prevention and control--Juvenile literature. | Survival--
   Juvenile literature. | Paradise (Calif.)--History--Juvenile literature.
Classification: LCC SD421.23 .E27 2020 (print) |
   LCC SD421.23 (ebook) | DDC 363.34/909794--dc23
LC record available at https://lccn.loc.gov/2019053369
LC ebook record available at https://lccn.loc.gov/2019053370

Crabtree Publishing Company

www.crabtreebooks.com   1-800-387-7650

Printed in the U.S.A./022020/CG20200102

Published in Canada
Crabtree Publishing
616 Welland Ave.
St. Catharines, Ontario
L2M 5V6

Published in the United States
Crabtree Publishing
PMB 59051
350 Fifth Avenue, 59th Floor
New York, New York 10118

Published in the United Kingdom
Crabtree Publishing
Maritime House
Basin Road North, Hove
BN41 1WR

Published in Australia
Crabtree Publishing
3 Charles Street
Coburg North
VIC, 3058

Contents

Wildfires and Their Victims

Wildfires are dangerous, uncontrolled fires that burn in wild areas. They can be deadly, wiping out large areas of plants and killing wild animals. Sometimes, wildfires spread so far and so quickly that they reach places where people live. Then the victims of these terrible flames can be people too.

Deadly and Dangerous

Wildfires are extremely dangerous for people caught up near or in them. The air near a wildfire can be so hot that it can burn a person's skin. If someone gets too close to the fire, they can be seriously injured or die from severe burns.

Wildfires can cause terrible destruction to the landscape and people's property.

Most people are affected by wildfires not because of burns, but because of smoke. Smoke from wildfires can damage people's lungs if it is breathed in. It often contains poisons, such as **mercury vapor** and **carbon monoxide**, which can make a person extremely sick.

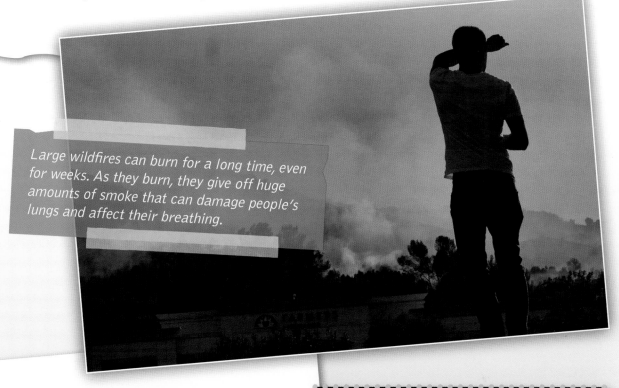

Large wildfires can burn for a long time, even for weeks. As they burn, they give off huge amounts of smoke that can damage people's lungs and affect their breathing.

Types of Wildfires

There are different types of wildfires depending on where they break out. The wildfires that occur in woodlands and forests are called forest fires. Fires that break out in areas of **grassland** and **scrub** are usually called bushfires. Some fires break out in places where there is a lot of **peat**, such as in Indonesia and other parts of Asia. Peat has material in it that easily catches fire, such as pieces of dead plant that have not rotted away.

TONI'S STORY

In this book, you can find out what it is like to live through a **natural disaster** by reading the **fictional** story of a young girl named Toni who was caught up in the Camp Fire wildfire disaster in Paradise, California. Look for her story on pages 6–7, 12–13, 16–17, 22–23, and 28–29.

TONI'S STORY:
Surviving Camp Fire

My name is Toni Robertson. I am 13 years old, and I'm from Paradise, California. That is, I used to live there—before the wildfire came. Paradise was such a cool place to live—it pretty much was paradise! I loved our house. It was on the edge of town, but I could still walk from there to my school. On the weekends, I hung out with my friends or went hiking with my mom and dad in the forest nearby.

Everything changed on Thursday, November 8, 2018, though. I'll always remember that date. I remember it being really hot and really dry too—we'd had hardly any rain for months, and the leaves on the ground crunched and crackled when you walked on them.

Paradise was a mountain town with a population of about 27,000 people. Some of those people were still in bed when the fire hit on the morning of November 8.

The first I knew of the wildfire was in the morning that day. I was at home, about to leave for school. Mom was in the kitchen, finishing up the breakfast stuff and packing her bag to get ready for work. Dad wasn't at home. He was out of town, working in Arizona on a sales trip. When the phone rang, Mom almost didn't answer it—we were already late for school and work. But I'm so glad now that she did. It was Uncle Greg. I could tell his voice sounded kind of worried, so I stopped by the door and waited to find out what was happening. Mom turned really pale when Greg spoke to her, and I could tell something bad was happening.

As soon as Mom got off the phone, she told me we had to leave—and fast. I was freaking out and asking her why, but all she said was, "It's a wildfire. We have to go."

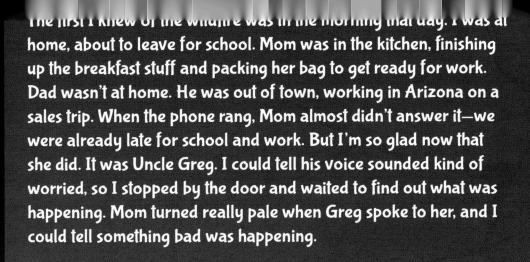

Looking back, I realize now that Paradise was like a tinderbox—all it needed was just one strike of a match...

DANGER

Trails of Destruction

Unable to outrun a wildfire, both people and animals caught up in the disaster often die.

Wildfires can be disastrous—not only for the landscape where they start, but also for people and animals that live there. Some animals, such as birds and deer, may be able to fly away or outrun a wildfire. But other animals, such as snakes and **livestock**, may be burned alive if they are caught up in the flames.

Changing Lives

Wildfires can change people's lives by changing the landscapes where they live. If the flames reach buildings, they can rip through wooden boards and **beams**. They can melt plastic and metal too. Vehicles, bridges, and railroad tracks can all be destroyed. If wildfires reach roads, they can even melt the surface of them, making them unusable.

Fast–Moving Flames

Wildfires will burn as long as there is something to burn. And they can move incredibly quickly if the wind is behind them. In fact, some wildfires move at speeds of up to 14 miles per hour (23 kph). It is not just the speed of a wildfire that can make it so dangerous. Sometimes, sparks from wildfire flames can travel many feet across the ground, quickly starting another wildfire in the spot where they land.

BURNED TO NEAR EXTINCTION

In 2019-2020, wildlife experts feared up to a billion animals—including kangaroos, **wombats**, birds, reptiles, insects, livestock, and pets—were killed in massive wildfires that burned throughout Australia. The fires destroyed so much wildlife habitat that some species, such as the green carpenter bee and the glossy black cockatoo, may have been wiped out or are in danger of extinction.

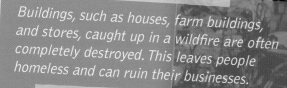

Buildings, such as houses, farm buildings, and stores, caught up in a wildfire are often completely destroyed. This leaves people homeless and can ruin their businesses.

After the Fire

Even when a wildfire is brought under control or burns itself out, it leaves behind a terrible scene. Miles of black, burned land is often the mark of a wildfire. **Charred** trees and buildings, as well as mounds of ash, scar the landscape. The entire area that a wildfire covered can stay hot for a long time after it has burned out. And it is then that people have the difficult job of cleaning up the mess and rebuilding their lives.

9

How Wildfires Work

All wildfires need three ingredients to start: **oxygen**, **fuel**, and heat. When these three factors are in place, a **chemical reaction** takes place that causes a fire to start.

A Dangerous Reaction

In a wildfire, oxygen combines with fuel. The fuel might be the dry grasses and plants of grassland or scrubland, or the **parched** plants and trees of a forest. In areas such as Indonesia, it can also be the peaty soil. When oxygen and fuel meet, all they need is heat to start the flames.

The Heat Factor

Heat is the third important factor in the chemical reaction. Wildfires start because the high temperature in the area has made the fuel, such as twigs and leaves, very dry and warm. This means that they catch fire easily. Heat also helps the fire grow bigger and hotter once it has started.

In forest fires where the trees are very tall, the flames can grow dangerously tall and hot.

Sky-High Flames

Heat is a major problem in forest fires, where fires can become incredibly hot because of the height of their fuel—the trees. In an area of small trees, once the flames grow to just 3 feet high (91 cm), they can reach temperatures of 1,472 °Fahrenheit (800 °C). That is twice as hot as a pizza oven!

As Hot as the Sun

In forests where trees have grown very tall, fires are even more deadly. When the flames reach 165 feet (50 m) high, they can burn at a heat of 2,192 °Fahrenheit (1,200 °C). That is almost one-quarter the temperature of the surface of the Sun!

Firefighters rely on important firefighting equipment, such as powerful hoses, to put out wildfires.

VICTIMS OF THE FIRE WALL

Oxygen is not only an important factor in wildfire chemical reactions. A lack of it in the air can be disastrous for firefighters trying to battle blazes. For example, in 1987 in China, firefighters were tackling a huge forest fire. The fire was so fierce that it moved forward in a giant wall of flames.

The fire wall moved so quickly and was burning at such high temperatures that it sucked all the oxygen from the air in front of it. With no available oxygen, the fuel in the firefighters' fire engines could not burn. The engines stopped working, which meant that the firefighters' hoses stopped working too. It was then impossible to put out the fire.

TONI'S STORY:
Fleeing Paradise

After we got the phone call, I did what Mom told me to do and grabbed a bag with my cell phone, a flashlight, and water. Mom had been near a wildfire when she was a girl, and they terrified her. I wanted to get out of the house and away from danger—fast.

Mom started up the car, and we drove down the street. It was 7:45 a.m. I couldn't see any sign of danger yet, but I knew fires could spread really quickly once they got going. Mom said we needed to head south, away from the fire, which was blowing downwind from Feather River Canyon. She said that we'd go to her sister's, who lived in Sacramento, and stay with her for a few days until it was safe to go home again.

People had to drive through fire and thick smoke.

As we got near the main roads, we started to see more cars moving south. It was 8:30 a.m. I got a call from my friend Jen. She was in the car with her family heading out of Paradise too. Jen sounded really scared. She told me that she could see flames behind her and that some of the houses in nearby streets had caught fire. I told her not to worry and to just keep on heading out of there. I said I'd meet her later, once we were all safe. They were heading for Sacramento, just like us.

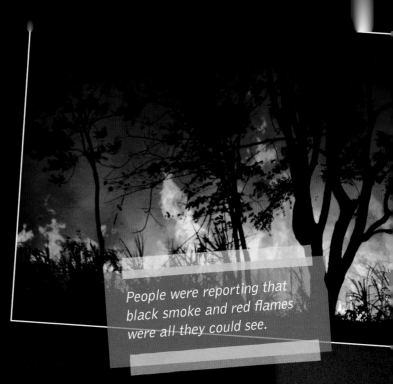

People were reporting that black smoke and red flames were all they could see.

But when I turned on the radio, I realized how bad things were getting. The reporter said that there was chaos on the highways as people tried to escape. Many vehicles had crashed into other cars, and some drove off **embankments**. Smoke had filled the sky and turned day to night. I got really scared for Jen, who was way behind us now.

The Causes of Wildfires

Wildfires can be caused by events in nature, such as lightning strikes or volcanic **eruptions**. But they can also be caused by the actions of people. These include smoking cigarettes, making campfires, and using electrical machinery in areas where wildfires can break out. Natural or human-made, all of these activities can cause the spark that starts the flames of a wildfire.

The heat of a lightning bolt sometimes starts a wildfire if it hits dry vegetation.

VICTIMS OF SMOKING

In 2012, in Catalonia, Spain, a terrible wildfire broke out that destroyed 34,600 acres (14,000 hectares) of land. Two people died in the fire as they tried to escape it by jumping from cliffs into the sea. Fire investigators later found out that the fire had been caused by people smoking cigarettes in the area.

Caused by Nature

When lightning hits the ground, it can cause the fuel of dry grass, scrub, trees, or peat to suddenly catch fire. When volcanoes erupt, their hot **lava** flows spill out onto the land around them, setting fire to dry areas of vegetation. Huge burning balls of lava, called lava bombs, can also be hurled from volcanoes. When they land on a dry, parched area, the heat from the lava bombs can set it on fire.

Caused by People

When people purposefully start fires to cause damage, it is called arson. In the United States, up to one-fifth of fires are a result of arson. However, fires can also begin accidentally because of farming methods. To clear land, farmers use a slash-and-burn method. This is when farmers burn areas of vegetation so that the land it grows on can then be used for farming. Sometimes these fires spread to surrounding areas and cause a wildfire.

Sparks and Ash

Other human activity in wildfire-prone areas also causes fires. When people use electrical machinery in these places, tiny sparks can shoot off from the machines. When these sparks land on dry vegetation, they can cause it to catch fire. People also sometimes smoke cigarettes or have campfires in natural places. Particles of hot ash from cigarettes or sparks from campfires can cause surrounding vegetation to catch fire, and a wildfire can start.

This farmer is using the slash-and-burn method on his land in Thailand. Unfortunately, this could lead to a wildfire.

TONI'S STORY:
Safety in Sacramento

We drove and drove on the highway, determined to make it to Sacramento. It was clear that a lot of other people had the same idea as us—the highway was packed with cars, and frightened faces stared back at us from their windows.

When we got to Sacramento, we hurried to Aunt Chloe's house. She was waiting for us on the driveway and raced to the car to open the doors. She and Mom were both crying as they hugged each other. Aunt Chloe said she'd been so scared for us, and that the news reports on TV looked really bad.

We hurried inside with her and couldn't believe what we saw as we looked at the TV screen. The only pictures of Paradise were ones that had been taken by helicopter from a distance—and they showed an inferno of flames. Smoke was drifting for miles, flames were billowing, and it looked like the whole world was on fire. How could anyone still in Paradise have survived?

Drones flying over northern California to study the fire from the air showed a widespread scene of disaster. Even towns not near the fire were swamped with smoke.

The news reporter on TV started talking to a family who had escaped. They said the first they had known of the disaster was when they saw flames and lots of smoke in the distance. They said the sky got darker and darker, and—like us—they just grabbed a bag and ran.

As they fled in their car, they could see the poles that hold power lines catching fire behind them and falling to the ground. They were really scared that the poles might hit the car. They also saw people near their burning houses calling out for help, but there was nothing they could do but just keep on driving for their lives.

Mom called Dad on the phone to tell him we were OK. She cried as she told him what we had seen, but they were also tears of relief that at least we had survived.

This photograph of Paradise was taken by a satellite in space. It shows the area engulfed in flames and smoke billowing into the sky.

DANGER

Where Wildfires Happen

We know that wildfires happen in different types of landscape around the world, from the grasslands of Australia, for example, to the forests of North America. Wildfires are also a danger in the peat lands of Indonesia, in Asia. Wildfires will burn wherever there is fuel for them.

Wildfires Around the World

Although we often hear about fires in Australia, Canada, and the United States, wildfires occur in many other places around the world. There have been terrible fires in European countries, such as Russia, Portugal, and France. There have also been wildfires in parts of China. Wildfires also burn in the grasslands of South Africa, and they have blazed in Chile and Bolivia in South America too.

Wildfires can even break out in some places where you would never imagine a wildfire could occur, such as in rain forests. In the first half of 2019, more than 87,000 fires were recorded in Brazil, in the Amazon rain forest. Some rain forests have eucalyptus trees, the leaves of which are filled with oils that easily burn. If a fire starts near a eucalyptus tree, the tree can catch fire quickly.

Bushfires in Australia can leave a charred landscape behind.

Weather and Wildfires

Wildfires only break out if conditions in a place make it possible. Wildfires happen in areas when they experience a lot of hot, dry weather. These weather conditions make vegetation crisp and dry—perfect fuel for a fire.

Dangerous Drought

Drought is a great danger in areas that experience wildfires. When an area has a long period of hot, dry weather with little or no rain, it is called a drought. Drought makes the land and plants in a place dry and warm. They then catch fire much more easily if touched by a spark.

Wildfires often happen in the grasslands of Africa because winds and high temperatures make the area prone to fire.

VICTIMS OF THE TREES

In 2017, Chile experienced a series of terrible wildfires that killed 11 people and burned 2,200 square miles (5,700 square km) of land. One of the reasons the fires spread so easily was that a lot of eucalyptus trees had been planted in the area, and the oil in their leaves fueled the devastating fires.

Dangerous Times

Australia has specially trained firefighters to help deal with wildfires during fire season, such as this crew in Tumut, New South Wales.

Wildfires can occur wherever the conditions are right for them, but they are more common in certain parts of the world and at certain times of the year. These are called fire seasons, and they occur at times of the year when the weather is hot and dry.

The Season for Fire

Fire seasons take place at different times around the world. From June to October, North American grassland and forest wildfires are most likely to occur due to hot, dry weather during the summer season. California is particularly at risk of wildfires during its hot summer season. Meanwhile, in southeast Australia, bushfires usually take place between December and March, when the weather there is at its driest. In northern Australia, fires are common between April and September, when it is hot and dry.

Fires in Asia

In India, the typical wildfire season is from January to June. After this, there are heavy **monsoon** rains, which help put out any fires and prevent new ones from starting. But wildfires are also possible in the fall, when hot, dry winds inland blow toward the coast, helping to spread fires.

In Indonesia, wildfires break out more often in the dry season, which is between January and May. Farmers in Indonesia often use fire to clear natural vegetation from the land so that they can use it for crop planting or for raising livestock. The farmers' use of fire is especially dangerous during the dry season and often leads to wildfires.

VICTIMS OF THE PEAT

In 2015, Indonesia was badly damaged by wildfires caused by the slash-and-burn technique of clearing land that is used there. The clearing left a lot of peat **exposed**. This, combined with a period of dry weather, caused terrible wildfires. The fires killed 19 people. Since 2015, more than half a million people have suffered from breathing conditions caused by **pollution** from the fires.

The smoke from wildfires, such as this one in Java, Indonesia, can have a terrible effect on people's health.

21

TONI'S STORY:
Paradise No More

Over the next few days, Mom and I were in a state of shock. Aunt Chloe looked after us, bringing us food and iced tea, and giving us lots of big hugs. She could see how upset we were. Then, finally, something good happened—I got a call from Jen.

Jen told me that she had gotten out of Paradise just in time, and she and her family had made it to her grandparents' house in Sacramento. Like us, they couldn't believe what they'd seen on the news. Jen came over to Aunt Chloe's house, and we cried and hugged each other. We were both so devastated by what we had seen.

DANGER

Cars and other vehicles were so badly burned that often just a mangled shell remained. In some cases, the metal was entirely melted.

Next, Dad flew in to Sacramento. Aunt Chloe took me and Mom to meet him at the airport. I raced up to him as soon as I saw him, and Dad lifted me up and hugged me so tight I couldn't breathe.

Over the next few weeks, more news came through about Paradise. When the firefighters finally got the flames under control, they had been able to go into the town to see how bad the damage was. News reporters followed, and the pictures they showed were terrible. Buildings had been completely destroyed and there were blackened remains of vehicles everywhere. It was so sad to see.

All that remained of some buildings in Paradise were their concrete stairs.

A month after the fire we were told that we could go back to Paradise to see what was left of our home and the town. When we got there, it was as bad as we had feared—like a scene from a war movie.

Our home was just a pile of rubble—and every single thing that had been in my bedroom was burned to dust. It was all gone! Every other home on our street was just a charred mess too. And my school was completely destroyed. The convenience store was gone, and all the shops and restaurants we used to go to were wrecked. Mom, Dad, and I decided then and there that there was nothing left for us in Paradise now. We knew we'd have to start all over again somewhere else. It felt like my whole world had ended.

How Science Can Fight Wildfires

The earlier a wildfire can be spotted, the sooner people and animals can be moved to safety. That is why scientists are constantly working to come up with new technology that will help them **predict** wildfires.

Climate Change and Wildfires

Scientists are studying **climate change** to find out how it is affecting wildfires around the world. In some places, climate change is causing drier weather. This is leading to more droughts, and they are lasting longer. Scientists who study weather, called meteorologists, have seen that this has resulted in many more wildfires in a number of places.

Climate change is believed to be causing wildfires outside of the fire season. The Rhea wildfire broke out in grassland in Oklahoma in April 2018 after an unusually dry winter.

VICTIMS OF THE WEATHER

Scientists also study past weather to learn more about wildfires. For example, they know that the "Black Saturday" wildfires in Australia in 2009 followed record-breaking summer temperatures. In these terrible fires, 173 people were killed and 7,500 were left homeless.

Weather satellites in space also pick up weather conditions on Earth that might lead to wildfires.

California Crisis

One of the areas affected by drier weather is California, which now has a fire season that is 78 days longer than it was in the 1970s. This is due to drier winters, warmer springs, and hotter summers.

Taking Pictures

Scientists also study the photos of wildfire-prone areas taken by the onboard **infrared** cameras of airplanes, helicopters, and drones that regularly fly over danger zones during fire seasons. A number of photos are taken by the cameras at regular **intervals**. The photographs are then loaded into computer programs. The systems compare the photographs and note any changes in heat that show up on the infrared images. If a marked increase in heat is shown, scientists know that the area is at risk of a wildfire.

On the Lookout

Some forests that are in wildfire-prone places also have special fire lookout towers that are used to regularly check for fires. In these towers are webcams that record images of the area. The images are fed to control centers, where people study them for signs of fire. The towers also have **sensors** that can pick up infrared **radiation**, which is given off when an area becomes hot and starts to burn. Some sensors also pick up changes in the air, such as reduced moisture or smoke caused by fire.

Protecting People

The best way to protect people from wildfires is to try to prevent them from happening. Governments in areas that have a lot of wildfires try to educate people who live there about how best to manage the land to prevent wildfires, and how to protect themselves if a fire does break out.

The darker area of ground near the road in this image is a firebreak. It has been deliberately set on fire to break or stop a wildfire's progress and keep it from reaching the road.

Starting Little Fires

One way to help prevent future wildfires is to set small fires, called controlled burns. Burning away any **flammable** vegetation near buildings or roads creates a gap of bare ground, called a firebreak. This keeps a wildfire from spreading.

Letting Small Fires Burn

If firefighters put out every single wildfire, it would result in a buildup of dead trees and plants that might otherwise have burned in natural fires. This buildup of dry plants is **potential** fuel for a wildfire. Burning these areas of dead vegetation in small controlled fires helps prevent this buildup.

Getting Rid of Dead Wood

Forest managers can also help control fires by cutting dead branches from trees. Dead wood is drier and more likely to burn than living wood, which contains more water. It also helps to cut back **overlapping** tree branches to keep fires from spreading from branch to branch and tree to tree.

If the Worst Happens...

People in wildfire danger zones should keep a disaster supply kit ready in case a fire breaks out. This might include a radio for hearing the latest news, water, a first aid kit, and breathing masks.

PROTECTING POTENTIAL VICTIMS

It is also important for people living in wildfire danger zones to listen for any warnings of potential fires. Warnings are usually given on the radio, television, or Internet. In the United States, for example, a Fire Weather Watch is a warning that tells people that the weather in the next 24 hours could lead to wildfires. A Red Flag Warning tells people that a wildfire is likely to break out.

This fire rating sign in Marysville, Australia, warns people of the likelihood of wildfires during its fire season.

FIRE DANGER RATING TODAY

VERY HIGH · SEVERE · EXTREME · HIGH · LOW-MODERATE · CODE RED

PREPARE. ACT. SURVIVE

TONI'S STORY:
Life after the Fire

When we returned from Paradise to Sacramento, we were in shock because of what we had seen. We had prepared ourselves to expect the worst, but none of us had imagined how lost we'd feel after seeing our homes and town destroyed.

Aunt Chloe was wonderful—she said we could stay with her as long as we liked. Dad's bosses have been great too. They said he could continue working from Sacramento and that they would give us as much support as they could while we looked for a new home.

A few months later, we moved out of Aunt Chloe's house into a rented apartment. It is now six months since the disaster and we are finally starting to feel more settled. I have started going to a new school and have new friends. I also see Jen whenever I can.

Climate change is affecting the weather in California, making it hotter and drier for longer periods of time. Many people believe this will lead to more wildfires in the future.

Mom, Dad, and I have realized that we are the lucky ones. Some of our neighbors never made it out of the fire. They died in their homes or in their cars, trying to escape. Many others who did make it out are still living in temporary housing—the hotels and motels all over Northern California are full of people who have lost their homes.

The fire has changed everything for me, just like it changed everything for Mom when she was a little girl. I am really scared of wildfires now because I've learned they can break out so quickly.

Jen and I spoke about our fears, and we have decided to try and raise **awareness** about the dangers of wildfires. We tell all our friends about the importance of being prepared. You have to have an escape plan. You also need to keep a survival bag ready at all times, and put it somewhere you can grab it instantly when needed. We have also started an online support group for the young survivors of Paradise, so we can all talk about how we feel and try to help each other. I hope that, together, we can learn to process what has happened to us and rebuild our lives.

These flowers were planted outside a home in Paradise. They symbolize the hope of its residents that they can rebuild their lives there.

DANGER

Glossary

awareness Being aware of, or thinking about, something

beams Large pieces of wood that are used to hold up parts of buildings

carbon monoxide A gas that can be poisonous to humans and animals

charred Burned so that it is blackened and crumbling

chemical reaction A reaction that takes place between two or more chemicals

climate change The long-term change in Earth's weather patterns

drones Unmanned vehicles that can be controlled by people far away

embankments Raised banks or walls that are built to carry a road or hold back water

engulfed Completely swallowed up or covered by something

eruptions Explosions

exposed Uncovered and vulnerable

fictional Made up, not true

flammable Able to easily burst into flames

fuel A substance that provides things with energy

grassland An area of land in which tall grasses grow

infrared A type of heat energy that can be seen with special technology

intervals Spaced-out periods of time

lava Hot liquid rock

livestock Farmed, not wild, animals

mercury vapor The form that the substance mercury takes when it turns into a gas

monsoon A wind in Asia that brings heavy rain and flooding

natural disaster A disaster caused by nature, not human-made

overlapping Extending over and covering part of something else

oxygen A gas found in air and water

parched Very dry and lacking water

peat Soil that contains a lot of rotting plants

pollution Dangerous gases and materials that are released into the air, water, and soil by human activities such as coal burning

potential Something that might be possible in the future

predict To say when something will happen

radiation The transmission, or giving off, of energy

satellite A human-made object that sends information from space back to Earth

scrub Very dry, woody plants that grow in hot places

sensors Tools that sense, or "feel," things

tinderbox A box that holds materials that can be used to start a fire easily

wombats Animals that live in Australia and that look like small bears

Learning More

Learn more about wildfires and their dangers.

Books

Burns, Kylie. *Wildfire Readiness*. Crabtree Publishing, 2019.

Seigel, Rachel. *California and Other Western Wildfires*. Crabtree Publishing, 2019.

Simon, Seymour. *Wildfires*. HarperCollins, 2016.

Thiessen, Mark. *Extreme Wildfire: Smoke Jumpers, High-Tech Gear, Survival Tactics, and the Extraordinary Science of Fire*. National Geographic Children's Books, 2016.

Websites

Learn more about wildfires and their causes at:
https://easyscienceforkids.com/all-about-wildfires

Find out about wildfires and how to prevent human-made wildfires at:
smokeybear.com/en

Watch National Geographic videos about forest fires at:
video.nationalgeographic.com/search?q=forest+fire

Discover more about forest fires at:
www.ducksters.com/science/earth_science/forest_fires.php

Index

About the Author

Sarah Eason has written many children's books, including books about science, geography, art, and history. She enjoys researching subjects such as natural disasters and finding out about the science behind these phenomenal events.